THE BOOK

teen sampler

Tyndale House
Publishers, Inc.
WHEATON, ILLINOIS

Contents

What is THE BOOK FOR TEENS?

DO YOU HAVE QUESTIONS about life, friends, family, God, or your future? If so, *The Book for Teens* is for you!

What is *The Book for Teens*? *The Book for Teens* is the Bible—the world's all-time best-seller. It is the most-read book in history! Many thousands of people just like you find their lives more meaningful because of the message in the Bible. People in all parts of the world turn to it to find answers.

You won't believe all the problems and questions *The Book for Teens* can help you with. Things like:

Does God really care about me?

The Bible is really a library of books. It's filled with stories about real people. It has great poetry and beautiful songs. It has prophecies and promises. And it is the true story of God's visiting our earth through his Son, Jesus Christ.

As you read about Jesus, you will discover the most terrific friend you could ever have—someone who's around twenty-four hours a day, anytime you need him!

We've put together this sampler from *The Book for Teens* so that you can get a taste of the great material that it holds. You'll be amazed at how *The Book for Teens* will speak to you! Get *The Book for Teens.* It could be the most important and life-changing step you will ever take.

The Message of *The Book for Teens*

The Bible begins by telling how the eternal God created the world and everything in it. He gave people a beautiful place to live and supplied everything they needed. Best of all, he was their friend.

That glorious beginning, however, was ruined when people disobeyed God and plunged into rebellion and sin. This broke humanity's relationship with God and brought judgment and death to the earth, its creatures, and humanity itself. Even so, God did not abandon his disobedient creatures; he set out to reclaim fallen people.

The Old Testament promises that a special individual would come, providing salvation for his people. That special individual, the Messiah, was to be "Immanuel" (Isaiah 7:14; 8:8), which in Hebrew means "God is with us." The Messiah would be both God and man. Those prophecies were fulfilled in the person of Jesus Christ.

When Jesus died to pay the penalty for our sin, he also removed all guilt produced by that sin and restored the broken relationship between God and humanity. He lives today and speaks continually to God on our behalf. "Therefore he is able, once and forever, to save everyone who comes to God through him" (Hebrews 7:24).

THE BOOK

FOR

TEENS

talks about life

... MY PURPOSE IS TO GIVE LIFE IN ALL ITS FULLNESS. John 10:10

complaining Is it OK to complain sometimes?

The Bible says complaining is wrong. When we complain, we fail to show appreciation for what God has done. Complaining builds attitudes of resentment and bitterness. When people around you complain, don't join in. Instead, remember God's faithfulness.

2Don't copy the behavior and customs of this world, but let God transform you into a new person by changing the way you think. . . . ROMANS 12:2

14In everything you do, stay away from complaining and arguing. PHILIPPIANS 2:14

9Don't grumble about each other, my brothers and sisters, or God will judge you. . . . JAMES 5:9

criticism I don't like people telling me what I need to change.

We'd all rather be praised than criticized! But rather than becoming angry and resentful at what people say, take the opportunity to grow and to become a better person. Others' criticism can help you become wise—and wisdom will make your life more productive and joyful.

[31]If you listen to constructive criticism, you will be at home among the wise.[32]If you reject criticism, you only harm yourself; but if you listen to correction, you grow in understanding. PROVERBS 15:31-32

[15]Fools think they need no advice, but the wise listen to others. PROVERBS 12:15

[5]It is better to be criticized by a wise person than to be praised by a fool! ECCLESIASTES 7:5

discouragement I'm discouraged.

No matter how bad your situation, you don't have to be down in the dumps. Why? Because Jesus says you can trust God, the Comforter. God is the only one who can comfort you totally, even in the midst of trouble and discouraging situations. And then, as you are comforted, you can pass that same comfort on to others who are discouraged, too.

[3]All praise to the God and Father of our Lord Jesus Christ. He is the source of every mercy and the God who comforts us. [4]He comforts us in all our troubles so that we can comfort others. When others are troubled, we will be able to give them the same comfort God has given us. 2 CORINTHIANS 1:3-4

¹⁸The LORD is close to the brokenhearted;
he rescues those who are crushed in spirit.

PSALM 34:18

¹⁹The thought of my suffering and homelessness is bitter beyond words. ²⁰I will never forget this awful time, as I grieve over my loss. ²¹Yet I still dare to hope when I remember this: ²²The unfailing love of the LORD never ends! By his mercies we have been kept from complete destruction. ²³Great is his faithfulness; his mercies begin afresh each day. ²⁴I say to myself, "The LORD is my inheritance; therefore, I will hope in him!" LAMENTATIONS 3:19-24

gossip Sometimes I gossip.

If you're careless with what you say, you can't take your words back. It's better to think before you speak. Ask God to change your heart so that instead of tearing people down, you can build people up with what you say.

⁵So also, the tongue is a small thing, but what enormous damage it can do. A tiny spark can set a great forest on fire. JAMES 3:5

²⁰Fire goes out for lack of fuel, and quarrels disappear when gossip stops. PROVERBS 26:20

²⁶If you claim to be religious but don't control your tongue, you are just fooling yourself, and your religion is worthless. JAMES 1:26

guilt I have a guilty conscience.

How can you keep your conscience clear? Treasure your faith in Christ more than anything else, and do what is right. As you walk with God, he'll speak to you, letting you know the difference between right and wrong. And if you do stray, confess your sin to God, and you will be forgiven (see "Forgiveness," page 46).

¹⁹Cling tightly to your faith in Christ, and always keep your conscience clear. For some people have deliberately violated their consciences; as a result, their faith has been shipwrecked.

1 TIMOTHY 1:19

⁹Don't keep looking at my sins.
Remove the stain of my guilt.
¹⁰Create in me a clean heart, O God.
Renew a right spirit within me.

PSALM 51:9-10

⁷Let the people turn from their wicked deeds. Let them banish from their minds the very thought of doing wrong! Let them turn to the LORD that he may have mercy on them. Yes, turn to our God, for he will abundantly pardon. ISAIAH 55:7

laziness I love to sleep in.

Those last few moments of sleep are wonderful: you lie in bed and don't want to get up because you're so warm and comfortable. But Proverbs warns against laziness. This doesn't mean you should never rest, but it does mean you should work hard for God—or else you may miss the good things he has planned for you.

¹³If you love sleep, you will end in poverty. Keep your eyes open, and there will be plenty to eat!

PROVERBS 20:13

⁴Lazy people are soon poor; hard workers get rich.

PROVERBS 10:4

[14]As a door turns back and forth on its hinges, so the lazy person turns over in bed. PROVERBS 26:14

leadership How can I be a good example to my classmates?

If you want your friends to respect you and each other, how do you start? By treating them well. If you want someone to be honest, be sure *you* live that way. Then you'll earn the right to be heard, and lives will be changed—for the good.

[6]... encourage the young men to live wisely in all they do. [7]And you yourself must be an example to them by doing good deeds of every kind. Let everything you do reflect the integrity and seriousness of your teaching. TITUS 2:6-7

[7]... you yourselves became an example to all the Christians in Greece. 1 THESSALONIANS 1:7

[12]Be careful how you live among your unbelieving neighbors. Even if they accuse you of doing wrong, they will see your honorable behavior, and they will believe and give honor to God when he comes to judge the world. 1 PETER 2:12

life purpose Could I really make a difference in the world?

No matter where God has placed you, he's put you there for a purpose. So instead of thinking you're not "big enough" to make a difference, just do what you know you should. Ask God to direct you, and watch him accomplish great things through you!

¹Then the LORD told Abram, "Leave your country, your relatives, and your father's house, and go to the land that I will show you. ²I will cause you to become the father of a great nation. I will bless you and make you famous, and I will make you a blessing to others." GENESIS 12:1-2

⁶God has given each of us the ability to do certain things well. . . . ROMANS 12:6

²¹For to me, living is for Christ, and dying is even better. ²²Yet if I live, that means fruitful service for Christ. I really don't know which is better.
PHILIPPIANS 1:21-22

loneliness Sometimes I feel alone in the world.

Everyone experiences periods of loneliness. Sometimes we feel lonely even when we are surrounded by crowds of people! But you are never really alone: God is with you. He will be your refuge from life's storms, including the lonely times. He will fill the lonely void in your life if you reach out to him in prayer. He'll be your friend even if no one else will.

⁴But to the poor, O LORD, you are a refuge from the storm. To the needy in distress, you are a shelter from the rain and the heat. ⁸. . . The Sovereign LORD will wipe away all tears. He will remove forever all insults and mockery against his land and people. The LORD has spoken! ISAIAH 25:4, 8

¹⁰Even if my father and mother abandon me,
the LORD will hold me close. PSALM 27:10

[10]Don't be afraid, for I am with you. Do not be dismayed, for I am your God. I will strengthen you. I will help you. I will uphold you with my victorious right hand. ISAIAH 41:10

money **Is there anything wrong with making lots of money?**

There's nothing wrong with making money—unless you think it'll bring you happiness. Then you'll only crave more. To keep away from "loving" money, remember that one day your riches will be gone. Be content with what you have, and don't forget to share with others.

[10]For the love of money is at the root of all kinds of evil. And some people, craving money, have wandered from the faith and pierced themselves with many sorrows. 1 TIMOTHY 6:10

[11]. . . I have learned how to get along happily whether I have much or little. [12]I know how to live on almost nothing or with everything. I have learned the secret of living in every situation, whether it is with a full stomach or empty, with plenty or little.
PHILIPPIANS 4:11-12

[5]So put to death the sinful, earthly things lurking within you. Have nothing to do with sexual sin, impurity, lust, and shameful desires. Don't be greedy for the good things of this life, for that is idolatry.
COLOSSIANS 3:5

possessions I don't have much money or very many clothes.

The key to being happy with what you have is to keep your priorities straight and to be content with what God gives you—whether little or much. If you focus on what you're supposed to *do* rather than on what you *have or don't have*, you, too, will learn "how to get along happily."

11Not that I was ever in need, for I have learned how to get along happily whether I have much or little. 12I know how to live on almost nothing or with everything. I have learned the secret of living in every situation, whether it is with a full stomach or empty, with plenty or little. 13For I can do everything with the help of Christ who gives me the strength I need. PHILIPPIANS 4:11-13

25So I tell you, don't worry about everyday life— whether you have enough food, drink, and clothes. Doesn't life consist of more than food and clothing? 26Look at the birds. They don't need to plant or harvest or put food in barns because your heavenly Father feeds them. And you are far more valuable to him than they are. 27Can all your worries add a single moment to your life? Of course not.

MATTHEW 6:25-27

6Yet true religion with contentment is great wealth. 7After all, we didn't bring anything with us when we came into the world, and we certainly cannot carry anything with us when we die. 8So if we have enough food and clothing, let us be content. 9But people who long to be rich fall into temptation and are trapped by many foolish and harmful desires that plunge them into ruin and destruction. ¹⁰For the love of money is at the root of all kinds of evil. And some people, craving money, have wandered from the faith and pierced themselves with many sorrows.

1 TIMOTHY 6:6-10

reputation I try to work hard and be kind, but nobody seems to notice.

Ruth earned a great reputation. As a result Boaz noticed Ruth, helped to provide for her and her family, and later married her! Your reputation is formed by the people who watch you at school, at home, at church, and at work. If you're always kind and hardworking (no matter who's watching or not watching), you'll gain a good reputation, too.

¹⁰Ruth fell at his feet and thanked him warmly. "Why are you being so kind to me?" she asked. "I am only a foreigner."

¹¹"Yes, I know," Boaz replied. "But I also know about the love and kindness you have shown your mother-in-law since the death of your husband. I have heard how you left your father and mother and your own land to live here among complete strangers." RUTH 2:10-11

¹My child, never forget the things I have taught you. Store my commands in your heart, ²for they will give you a long and satisfying life. ³Never let loyalty and kindness get away from you! Wear them like a necklace; write them deep within your heart. ⁴Then you will find favor with both God and people, and you will gain a good reputation. PROVERBS 3:1-4

15Work hard so God can approve you. Be a good worker, one who does not need to be ashamed and who correctly explains the word of truth.

2 TIMOTHY 2:15

satisfaction I never feel satisfied.

If you're longing for lasting satisfaction in your life, you won't find it at the mall or with the "in" crowd. Only God can satisfy your deepest longings. Ask him to help you long for him as you long for food when you're hungry and water when you're thirsty. Put God first in your life, and he will help you discover what can truly satisfy.

1 O God, you are my God;
I earnestly search for you.
my whole body longs for you
where there is no water.
2 I have seen you in your sanctuary
and gazed upon your power and glory.
3 Your unfailing love is better to me than life itself;
how I praise you! PSALM 63:1-3

1 The LORD is my shepherd;
I have everything I need.
2 He lets me rest in green meadows;
he leads me beside peaceful streams.
3   He renews my strength.
He guides me along right paths,
bringing honor to his name.
4 Even when I walk
through the dark valley of death,
for you are close beside me.
protect and comfort me.
5 You prepare a feast for me

in the presence of my enemies.
anointing my head with oil.
My cup overflows with blessings.
⁶ *Surely your goodness and unfailing love will*
    pursue me
all the days of my life,
and I will live in the house of the LORD forever.

PSALM 23:1-6

⁴ *The one thing I ask of the LORD—*
    the thing I seek most—
is to live in the house of the LORD all the days of
    my life,
    delighting in the LORD's perfections
    and meditating in his Temple. PSALM 27:4

self-worth I wonder what I'm worth.

What are you worth? If you ask your friends, they
might evaluate you according to what you do, what
you say, or how you look. But God values you highly
and cares for you immensely. If God cares for sparrows, certainly he cares much more for you, a creature
made in his image. To him, you're absolutely priceless!

⁶ *"What is the price of five sparrows? A couple of*
pennies? Yet God does not forget a single one of
them. ⁷ *And the very hairs on your head are all num-*
bered. So don't be afraid; you are more valuable to
him than a whole flock of sparrows. LUKE 12:6-7

²⁶ *Then God said, "Let us make people in our image,*
to be like ourselves. They will be masters over all
life—the fish in the sea, the birds in the sky, and all
the livestock, wild animals, and small animals."

27 So God created people in his own image;
God patterned them after himself;
male and female he created them.

PSALM 8:3-5

3 When I look at the night sky and see the work of
your fingers—
the moon and the stars you have set in place—
4 what are mortals that you should think of us,
mere humans that you should care for us?
5 For you made us only a little lower than God,
and you crowned us with glory and honor.

GENESIS 1:26-27

thoughts Does it really matter what I think about as long as I do what is right?

Jesus says that thinking about evil is just as bad as doing evil. Why? Because God looks at the condition of your heart, not just the things you do. Unclean thoughts pollute your heart and make you unacceptable to God, who is pure and holy. When your thoughts stray toward anything that's wrong, choose to turn them toward something good instead.

20 And then he added, "It is the thought-life that defiles you. 21 For from within, out of a person's heart, come evil thoughts, sexual immorality, theft, murder, 22 adultery, greed, wickedness, deceit, eagerness for lustful pleasure, envy, slander, pride, and foolishness. MARK 7:20-22

2 . . . let God transform you into a new person by changing the way you think. Then you will know what God wants you to do, and you will know how good and pleasing and perfect his will really is.

ROMANS 12:2

8 . . . Fix your thoughts on what is true and honorable and right. Think about things that are pure and lovely and admirable. Think about things that are excellent and worthy of praise. 9Keep putting into practice all you learned from me and heard from me and saw me doing, and the God of peace will be with you. PHILIPPIANS 4:8-9

~~work~~ ~~I work harder than everybody else.~~

Does anybody notice your hard work? God certainly does, and he will reward you! Hard work can pay off in other big ways, too: people notice you, you get a great reputation, you gain experience and knowledge, and you grow more mature spiritually. Most of all, when you're hard at work doing what pleases God, you will feel his pleasure and know your labor is pleasing to him. Just make sure you're working for him!

7Work with enthusiasm, as though you were working for the Lord rather than for people. EPHESIANS 6:7

29To those who use well what they are given, even more will be given, and they will have an abundance. But from those who are unfaithful, even what little they have will be taken away.

MATTHEW 25:29

28If you are a thief, stop stealing. Begin using your hands for honest work, and then give generously to others in need. EPHESIANS 4:28

worry I worry a lot.

If you worry constantly, try this cure: Remember that God cares about you, admit to him what you're worried about, and let other Christians help you. Instead of being controlled by what's happening to you, you can choose to trust God, who controls the world anyway!

7Give all your worries and cares to God, for he cares about what happens to you. 1 PETER 5:7

25"So I tell you, don't worry about everyday life— whether you have enough food, drink, and clothes. Doesn't life consist of more than food and clothing? 26Look at the birds. They don't need to plant or harvest or put food in barns because your heavenly Father feeds them. And you are far more valuable to him than they are. 27Can all your worries add a single moment to your life? Of course not.

MATTHEW 6:25-27

6Don't worry about anything; instead, pray about everything. Tell God what you need, and thank him for all he has done. 7If you do this, you will experience God's peace, which is far more wonderful than the human mind can understand. His peace will guard your hearts and minds as you live in Christ Jesus. PHILIPPIANS 4:6-7

THE BOOK

FOR

TEENS

talks about relationships

LET LOVE BE YOUR HIGHEST GOAL.

1 Corinthians 14:1

criticizing others — Sometimes I judge or criticize others.

It's so easy to pick on other people—while excusing your own faults. But did you know that we often criticize others for doing the same things we do ourselves? Instead of criticizing others, forgive them—just as Christ forgave you. The next time you open your mouth to judge someone, remember what Christ did for you. Then take a look at yourself. Maybe *you* need to change something?

7Stop judging others, and you will not be judged. Stop criticizing others, or it will all come back on you. If you forgive others, you will be forgiven.

LUKE 6:37

13You must make allowance for each other's faults and forgive the person who offends you. Remember, the Lord forgave you, so you must forgive others.

COLOSSIANS 3:13

11Don't speak evil against each other, my dear brothers and sisters. If you criticize each other and condemn each other, then you are criticizing and condemning God's law. But you are not a judge who can decide whether the law is right or wrong. Your job is to obey it. 12God alone, who made the law, can rightly judge among us. He alone has the power to save or to destroy. So what right do you have to condemn your neighbor? JAMES 4:11-12

forgiving others I can't forgive him/her for what he/she has done.

It's never easy to forgive. But God says we have to because he has forgiven us—Jesus, his Son, even forgave those who were executing him! If it's hard to forgive someone who's wronged you a little, remember that God has forgiven *you* for wronging him a lot. And he continues to forgive you. Ask him to help you forgive others that same way.

34Jesus said, "Father, forgive these people, because they don't know what they are doing." . . . LUKE 23:34

14If you forgive those who sin against you, your heavenly Father will forgive you. 15But if you refuse to forgive others, your Father will not forgive your sins. MATTHEW 6:14-15

21Then Peter came to him and asked, "Lord, how often should I forgive someone who sins against me? Seven times?"

22"No!" Jesus replied, "seventy times seven!"

MATTHEW 18:21-22

17Never pay back evil for evil to anyone. Do things in such a way that everyone can see you are honorable. 18Do your part to live in peace with everyone, as much as possible. ROMANS 12:17-18

13You must make allowance for each other's faults and forgive the person who offends you. Remember, the Lord forgave you, so you must forgive others.

COLOSSIANS 3:13

friendship Why do some people act like my friends when really they are not?

Some people pretend to be friends and will act friendly when they don't mean it. They may want to look good (being seen with the right people) or to gain something through the "friendship." Instead of looking for friendship from such people, we can look to Jesus. He will be our real friend. And we should treat others the way he treats us—with sincerity, love, and faithfulness. What kind of friend are you?

24There are "friends" who destroy each other, but a real friend sticks closer than a brother.

PROVERBS 18:24

1After David had finished talking with Saul, he met Jonathan, the king's son. There was an immediate bond of love between them, and they became the best of friends. 2From that day on Saul kept David with him at the palace and wouldn't let him return home. 3And Jonathan made a special vow to be David's friend, 4and he sealed the pact by giving him his robe, tunic, sword, bow, and belt. 1 SAMUEL 18:1-4

> ^{12}*It is not an enemy who taunts me—*
> *I could bear that.*
> *I could have hidden from them.*
> ^{13}*Instead, it is you—my equal,*
> *my companion and close friend.*
> ^{14}*What good fellowship we enjoyed*
> *as we walked together to the house of God.*
>
> PSALM 55:12-14

^{17}*A friend is always loyal, and a brother is born to help in time of need.* PROVERBS 17:17

love What does real love look like?

Just read 1 Corinthians 13 for a godly perspective on what real love looks like. It means always being patient and kind—and never jealous. It means thinking of others before yourself and not holding a grudge over their heads. It means not jumping all over another's case when you're having a bad day. Do you love people with that kind of love?

^{4}*Love is patient and kind. Love is not jealous or boastful or proud* ^{5}*or rude. Love does not demand its own way. Love is not irritable, and it keeps no record of when it has been wronged.* ^{6}*It is never glad about injustice but rejoices whenever the truth wins out.* ^{7}*Love never gives up, never loses faith, is always hopeful, and endures through every circumstance.*

1 CORINTHIANS 13:4-7

^{18}*"Never seek revenge or bear a grudge against anyone, but love your neighbor as yourself. I am the* LORD*."* LEVITICUS 19:18

^{31}*Do for others as you would like them to do for you.*

LUKE 6:31

prejudice Is it OK to treat some people better than others?

The Bible says no, you shouldn't show favoritism. That means you shouldn't agree with everything the popular kids say, and you shouldn't knock down what the "rejects" say. Treating certain people better than others is wrong. God loves all people exactly the same. James 2:1 says, "How can you claim that you have faith in our glorious Lord Jesus Christ if you favor some people more than others?" We must follow God's example by being perfectly fair to everyone.

16"I instructed the judges, 'You must be perfectly fair at all times, not only to fellow Israelites, but also to the foreigners living among you. 17When you make decisions, never favor those who are rich; be fair to lowly and great alike. Don't be afraid of how they will react, for you are judging in the place of God. Bring me any cases that are too difficult for you, and I will handle them.' " DEUTERONOMY 1:16-17

34Then Peter replied, "I see very clearly that God doesn't show partiality. 35In every nation he accepts those who fear him and do what is right."

ACTS 10:34–35

1My dear brothers and sisters, how can you claim that you have faith in our glorious Lord Jesus Christ if you favor some people more than others?

JAMES 2:1

THE BOOK

FOR

TEENS

talks about Hot Topics

THE LORD IS GOOD. WHEN TROUBLE COMES, HE IS A STRONG REFUGE. AND HE KNOWS EVERYONE WHO TRUSTS IN HIM.

Nahum 1:7

abortion   I'm considering having an abortion.

You didn't plan on getting pregnant; it "just happened." And all the sorrys in the world won't change the fact that you now have a baby inside you. You don't know what to do. Abortion seems like the easy way out because then nobody will know. But you'll know—and God will know. And God says *all* children are special, even if you didn't plan them. So choose to give your child life, and trust God to help you through any difficulty.

> [3] *Children are a gift from the LORD;*
> *they are a reward from him.*
>
> PSALM 127:3

^{13} You made all the delicate, inner parts of my body
  and knit me together in my mother's womb.
^{14} Thank you for making me so wonderfully complex!
  Your workmanship is marvelous—and how well
  I know it.
^{15} You watched me as I was being formed in utter
  seclusion,
  as I was woven together in the dark of the womb.
^{16} You saw me before I was born.
  Every day of my life was recorded in your book.
  before a single day had passed.
^{17} How precious are your thoughts about me, O God!
  They are innumerable!
^{18} I can't even count them;
  they outnumber the grains of sand!...

PSALM 139:13-18

^{5}"I knew you before I formed you in your mother's
womb. Before you were born I set you apart and
appointed you as my spokesman to the world."

JEREMIAH 1:5

drinking Is it OK to drink? My friends do.

Proverbs says those who drink will always have trouble—and they'll waste time they could be spending on something else that's better for them. These verses don't paint a pretty picture. After all, who'd want to look like that—or have those experiences? Alcohol dulls your judgment. You can lose control of what you're doing or where you are—the drink and the people you're drinking with are controlling you! God wants us to be controlled by his Spirit, not by alcohol.

²⁹Who has anguish? Who has sorrow? Who is always fighting? Who is always complaining? Who has unnecessary bruises? Who has bloodshot eyes? ³⁰It is the one who spends long hours in the taverns, trying out new drinks. PROVERBS 23:29-30

¹Wine produces mockers; liquor leads to brawls. Whoever is led astray by drink cannot be wise.

PROVERBS 20:1

²⁴Those who belong to Christ Jesus have nailed the passions and desires of their sinful nature to his cross and crucified them there. GALATIANS 5:24

¹⁸Don't be drunk with wine, because that will ruin your life. Instead, let the Holy Spirit fill and control you. EPHESIANS 5:18

evil Why is there evil in the world?

Why is the world so bad? It didn't start out that way when God created it. But because people chose to go their own way instead of God's, they began to do evil things. That's why even "good" people get hurt. But that doesn't mean God is powerless. He has acted and is acting for our good—even in the midst of evil.

²⁸When they refused to acknowledge God, he abandoned them to their evil minds and let them do things that should never be done. ²⁹Their lives became full of every kind of wickedness, sin, greed, hate, envy, murder, fighting, deception, malicious behavior, and gossip. ³⁰They are backstabbers, haters of God, insolent, proud, and boastful. They are forever inventing new ways of sinning and are disobedient to their parents. ³¹They refuse to understand, break their promises, and are heartless and unforgiving. ³²They are fully aware of God's death penalty for those who do these things, yet they go right ahead and do them anyway. And, worse yet, they encourage others to do them, too. ROMANS 1:28-32

⁴I will reject perverse ideas
and stay away from every evil. PSALM 101:4

¹⁹Do not fret because of evildoers; don't envy the wicked. ²⁰For the evil have no future; their light will be snuffed out. PROVERBS 24:19-20

homosexuality Is it OK to be gay?

There were homosexuals in Paul's day, too. But God forbids such behavior, saying it's not what he designed sex to be. His plan is one man, one woman, in marriage for a lifetime. If you have homosexual desires, you can and must resist acting on them. Ask God—and a trusted Christian counselor—for help.

²⁶That is why God abandoned them to their shameful desires. Even the women turned against the natural way to have sex and instead indulged in sex with each other. ²⁷And the men, instead of having normal sexual relationships with women, burned with lust for each other. Men did shameful things with other men and, as a result, suffered within themselves the penalty they so richly deserved.

ROMANS 1:26-27

²²"Do not practice homosexuality; it is a detestable sin. LEVITICUS 18:22

¹³The penalty for homosexual acts is death to both parties. They have committed a detestable act and are guilty of a capital offense. LEVITICUS 20:13

⁹Don't you know that those who do wrong will have no share in the Kingdom of God? Don't fool yourselves. Those who indulge in sexual sin, who are idol worshipers, adulterers, male prostitutes, homosexuals, ¹⁰thieves, greedy people, drunkards, abusers, and swindlers—none of these will have a share in the Kingdom of God. 1 CORINTHIANS 6:9-10

purity Is it OK to go to R-rated movies?

Your friends are pressuring you; your parents say no. What do you do? The Bible tells us to be careful what goes into our mind, for that's what will come out. Take a look at the list in Galatians 5:19-21. Compare it with 5:22-23. Which person would you rather be?

¹⁹When you follow the desires of your sinful nature, your lives will produce these evil results: sexual immorality, impure thoughts, eagerness for lustful pleasure, ²⁰idolatry, participation in demonic activities, hostility, quarreling, jealousy, outbursts of anger, selfish ambition, divisions, the feeling that everyone is wrong except those in your own little group, ²¹envy, drunkenness, wild parties, and other kinds of sin. Let me tell you again, as I have before, that anyone living that sort of life will not inherit the Kingdom of God. ²²But when the Holy Spirit controls our lives, he will produce this kind of fruit in us: love, joy, peace, patience, kindness, goodness, faithfulness, ²³gentleness, and self-control. Here there is no conflict with the law. GALATIANS 5:19-23

²⁰And then he added, "It is the thought-life that defiles you. ²¹For from within, out of a person's heart, come evil thoughts, sexual immorality, theft, murder, [22]adultery, greed, wickedness, deceit, eagerness for lustful pleasure, envy, slander, pride, and foolishness. MARK 7:20-22

[8]And now, dear brothers and sisters, let me say one more thing as I close this letter. Fix your thoughts on what is true and honorable and right. Think about things that are pure and lovely and admirable. Think about things that are excellent and worthy of praise. PHILIPPIANS 4:8

[12]And we are instructed to turn from godless living and sinful pleasures. We should live in this evil world with self-control, right conduct, and devotion to God, TITUS 2:12

sex I'm tempted to have sex. Everybody else does.

Take God's warning, and run away! Don't put yourself in situations where sex is even possible. And by the way, "everybody does it" is a big, fat lie. Remember that you can become like the ones who "do it" at any time, but they can never become like you—a virgin. Besides, if you *really* love someone, you want the best for them. And that means not going to bed with anybody until you're married (see Prov. 5:18-20).

[22]Run from anything that stimulates youthful lust. Follow anything that makes you want to do right. Pursue faith and love and peace, and enjoy the companionship of those who call on the Lord with pure hearts. 2 TIMOTHY 2:22

[32]But the man who commits adultery is an utter fool, for he destroys his own soul. PROVERBS 6:32

⁵So put to death the sinful, earthly things lurking within you. Have nothing to do with sexual sin, impurity, lust, and shameful desires. Don't be greedy for the good things of this life, for that is idolatry.

COLOSSIANS 3:5

¹Finally, dear brothers and sisters, we urge you in the name of the Lord Jesus to live in a way that pleases God, as we have taught you. You are doing this already, and we encourage you to do so more and more. ²For you remember what we taught you in the name of the Lord Jesus. ³God wants you to be holy, so you should keep clear of all sexual sin. ⁴Then each of you will control your body and live in holiness and honor—⁵not in lustful passion as the pagans do, in their ignorance of God and his ways.

1 THESSALONIANS 4:1-5

THE
BOOK
FOR
TEENS

talks about the future

I PRAY THAT YOUR HEARTS WILL BE
FLOODED WITH LIGHT SO THAT YOU CAN
UNDERSTAND THE WONDERFUL FUTURE
HE HAS PROMISED TO THOSE HE CALLED.
I WANT YOU TO REALIZE WHAT A RICH AND
GLORIOUS INHERITANCE HE HAS GIVEN TO
HIS PEOPLE. Ephesians 1:18

the end of the world What if the world ends?

It's not *if* the world will end, it's *when!* The present
earth won't last forever, because God will destroy it
when the time is right. But he also promises that
he'll create a new one (see Rev. 21–22 for a sneak
peek). We don't know exactly what it'll be like, but
we do know that those who trust God will live there
with him forever. Will you be there?

*12I watched as the Lamb broke the sixth seal, and
there was a great earthquake. The sun became as*

dark as black cloth, and the moon became as red as blood. ¹³Then the stars of the sky fell to the earth like green figs falling from trees shaken by mighty winds. ¹⁴And the sky was rolled up like a scroll and taken away. And all of the mountains and all of the islands disappeared. REVELATION 6:12-14

¹⁷And this world is fading away, along with everything it craves. But if you do the will of God, you will live forever. 1 JOHN 2:17

⁷The end of the world is coming soon. Therefore, be earnest and disciplined in your prayers. 1 PETER 4:7

eternal life Is it really possible to live forever?

Everyone will live forever; it's just a question of where. Do you want to live forever in blessing—or in punishment? If you don't believe Jesus Christ, God's Son, died for your sins, you'll go to hell (a place of eternal punishment) when you die. But if you've accepted Jesus Christ as your Savior, you'll live forever in heaven with him! Choose life, and enjoy the blessings of eternity.

¹⁶"For God so loved the world that he gave his only Son, so that everyone who believes in him will not perish but have eternal life." JOHN 3:16

²⁵Jesus told her, "I am the resurrection and the life. Those who believe in me, even though they die like everyone else, will live again." JOHN 11:25

²³For the wages of sin is death, but the free gift of God is eternal life through Christ Jesus our Lord.

ROMANS 6:23

heaven Is heaven for real?

Heaven is definitely real. Jesus' words show that the way to eternal life, though you can't see it, is as secure as God's unchanging love. Jesus has already prepared the way to heaven for you. If you've chosen to believe in him, your room's ready and waiting!

2"There are many rooms in my Father's home, and I am going to prepare a place for you. If this were not so, I would tell you plainly. 3When everything is ready, I will come and get you, so that you will always be with me where I am. 4And you know where I am going and how to get there." JOHN 14:2-4

13But we are looking forward to the new heavens and new earth he has promised, a world where everyone is right with God. 2 PETER 3:13

5All who are victorious will be clothed in white. I will never erase their names from the Book of Life, but I will announce before my Father and his angels that they are mine. REVELATION 3:5

3I heard a loud shout from the throne, saying, "Look, the home of God is now among his people! He will live with them, and they will be his people. God himself will be with them. 4He will remove all of their sorrows, and there will be no more death or sorrow or crying or pain. For the old world and its evils are gone forever." REVELATION 21:3-4

hell Is there really a hell?

Those who think there isn't a hell are fooling themselves. The Bible describes hell as a place of torment, where you're separated from God and people you love forever. But you don't have to go there, if you trust Christ as your Savior and follow him as your Lord.

22Finally, the beggar died and was carried by the angels to be with Abraham. The rich man also died and was buried, 23and his soul went to the place of the dead. There, in torment, he saw Lazarus in the far distance with Abraham.24The rich man shouted, "Father Abraham, have some pity! Send Lazarus over here to dip the tip of his finger in water and cool my tongue, because I am in anguish in these flames." 25But Abraham said to him, "Son, remember that during your lifetime you had everything you wanted, and Lazarus had nothing. So now he is here being comforted, and you are in anguish. 26And besides, there is a great chasm separating us. Anyone who wanted to cross over to you from here is stopped at its edge, and no one there can cross over to us."

LUKE 16:22-26

4For God did not spare even the angels when they sinned; he threw them into hell, in gloomy caves and darkness until the judgment day. 2 PETER 2:4

11And I saw a great white throne, and I saw the one who was sitting on it. The earth and sky fled from his presence, but they found no place to hide. 12I saw the dead, both great and small, standing before God's throne. And the books were opened, including the Book of Life. And the dead were judged according to the things written in the books, according to what they had done. 13The sea gave up the dead in it, and death and the grave gave up the dead in them. They were all judged according to their deeds. 14And death and the grave were thrown into the lake of fire. This is the second death—the lake of fire.

15And anyone whose name was not found recorded in the Book of Life was thrown into the lake of fire.

REVELATION 20:11-15

life after death What happens after death?

The Bible spells it out. If you're a Christian—if you've accepted Christ's sacrifice on the cross for you—you'll be resurrected, along with every other Christian. How can you know you'll be transformed—
given a body that will never die? Because Jesus was raised from the dead and is now in heaven. And the same power that raised Jesus will also raise us and give us eternal life. You don't have to die to know that!

3I passed on to you what was most important and what had also been passed on to me—that Christ died for our sins, just as the Scriptures said. 4He was buried, and he was raised from the dead on the third day, as the Scriptures said. 1 CORINTHIANS 15:3-4

51. . . let me tell you a wonderful secret God has revealed to us. Not all of us will die, but we will all be transformed. 52It will happen in a moment, in the blinking of an eye, when the last trumpet is blown. For when the trumpet sounds, the Christians who have died will be raised with transformed bodies. And then we who are living will be transformed so that we will never die. 53For our perishable earthly bodies must be transformed into heavenly bodies that will never die. 54When this happens . . . then at last the Scriptures will come true:

"Death is swallowed up in victory.
⁵⁵ O death, where is your victory?
O death, where is your sting?"

1 CORINTHIANS 15:51-55

²⁰But we are citizens of heaven, where the Lord Jesus Christ lives. And we are eagerly waiting for him to return as our Savior. ²¹He will take these weak mortal bodies of ours and change them into glorious bodies like his own, using the same mighty power that he will use to conquer everything, everywhere.

PHILIPPIANS 3:20-21

THE BOOK

FOR

TEENS

talks about Faith

LET YOUR ROOTS GROW DOWN INTO HIM
AND DRAW UP NOURISHMENT FROM HIM,
SO YOU WILL GROW IN FAITH, STRONG
AND VIGOROUS IN THE TRUTH YOU WERE
TAUGHT. LET YOUR LIVES OVERFLOW WITH
THANKSGIVING FOR ALL HE HAS DONE!

Colossians 2:7

the Bible Why do Christians talk about memorizing the Bible?

The Bible is God's inspired word. God guided the writers to record just what he wanted to say. The Bible is our guidebook (telling us how to live), our textbook (teaching us what to believe), our spotlight (showing us what God is like), and our shield (protecting us from sin). God has an important message for you in the Bible. You should read it, commit it to memory, and obey it.

*11I have hidden your word in my heart,
that I might not sin against you.* PSALM 119:11

15You have been taught the holy Scriptures from childhood, and they have given you the wisdom to receive the salvation that comes by trusting in Christ Jesus. 16All Scripture is inspired by God and is useful to teach us what is true and to make us realize what is wrong in our lives. It straightens us out and teaches us to do what is right. 17It is God's way of preparing us in every way, fully equipped for every good thing God wants us to do.

2 TIMOTHY 3:15-17

12For the word of God is full of living power. It is sharper than the sharpest knife, cutting deep into our innermost thoughts and desires. It exposes us for what we really are. 13Nothing in all creation can hide from him. Everything is naked and exposed before his eyes. This is the God to whom we must explain all that we have done. HEBREWS 4:12-13

16For we were not making up clever stories when we told you about the power of our Lord Jesus Christ and his coming again. We have seen his majestic splendor with our own eyes. . . .

19Because of that, we have even greater confidence in the message proclaimed by the prophets. Pay close attention to what they wrote, for their words are like a light shining in a dark place—until the day Christ appears and his brilliant light shines in your hearts. 20Above all, you must understand that no prophecy in Scripture ever came from the prophets themselves 21or because they wanted to prophesy. It was the Holy Spirit who moved the prophets to speak from God. 2 PETER 1:16, 19-21

confession of sin I've blown it. Can God forgive me?

If you want to have a clean conscience, confess your sins to God. That means, when you become aware of your sins, admit them to God as sin. But once you confess your sins, God forgives you and forgets them. You don't need to keep feeling guilty, and you don't need to ask God to forgive you for the same sin over and over. God has forgiven you! His forgiveness is wonderful and complete! And he's promised it to you.

⁸If we say we have no sin, we are only fooling ourselves and refusing to accept the truth. ⁹But if we confess our sins to him, he is faithful and just to forgive us and to cleanse us from every wrong.

1 JOHN 1:8-9

¹². . . the LORD says, "Turn to me now, while there is time! Give me your hearts. Come with fasting, weeping, and mourning. ¹³Don't tear your clothing in your grief; instead, tear your hearts." Return to the LORD your God, for he is gracious and merciful. He is not easily angered. He is filled with kindness and is eager not to punish you. JOEL 2:12-13

⁸Draw close to God, and God will draw close to you. Wash your hands, you sinners; purify your hearts, you hypocrites. ⁹Let there be tears for the wrong things you have done. Let there be sorrow and deep grief. Let there be sadness instead of laughter, and gloom instead of joy. ¹⁰When you bow down before the Lord and admit your dependence on him, he will lift you up and give you honor. JAMES 4:8-10

discernment How do I know if God is talking?

When you think you are hearing from God, it's smart to ask whether it is God talking or someone else. Here's a good way to tell: compare it to Scripture. Does what you're hearing match what the Bible says? If not, it's not God talking to you, and it's not God's truth. That's why it's so important to know the Bible. So read up! And let God's Spirit guide you.

13"When the Spirit of truth comes, he will guide you into all truth. He will not be presenting his own ideas; he will be telling you what he has heard. He will tell you about the future. 14He will bring me glory by revealing to you whatever he receives from me." JOHN 16:13-14

5If you need wisdom—if you want to know what God wants you to do—ask him, and he will gladly tell you. He will not resent your asking. JAMES 1:5

1Dear friends, do not believe everyone who claims to speak by the Spirit. You must test them to see if the spirit they have comes from God. For there are many false prophets in the world. 2This is the way to find out if they have the Spirit of God: If a prophet acknowledges that Jesus Christ became a human being, that person has the Spirit of God. 3If a prophet does not acknowledge Jesus, that person is not from God. . . . 1 JOHN 4:1-3

faith Why doesn't God answer sometimes?

Sometimes when you ask God why something's happening, he doesn't seem to answer. Why? Sometimes it isn't time for you to know. God may be saying,

"Will you trust me?" Ask him to help you trust him even when you don't understand.

15The Sovereign LORD, the Holy One of Israel, says, "Only in returning to me and waiting for me will you be saved. In quietness and confidence is your strength. But you would have none of it. ISAIAH 30:15

25The LORD is wonderfully good to those who wait for him and seek him. 26So it is good to wait quietly for salvation from the LORD. 27And it is good for the young to submit to the yoke of his discipline.
LAMENTATIONS 3:25-27

How do I know Jesus really rose from the dead?

More than five hundred people saw him! With all those eyewitnesses, you know Jesus' resurrection is true. If it weren't, why would his followers have the courage, as many of them did, to die for their faith? You can be sure Jesus *did* rise from the dead.

1Early on Sunday morning, as the new day was dawning, Mary Magdalene and the other Mary went out to see the tomb. 2Suddenly there was a great earthquake, because an angel of the Lord came down from heaven and rolled aside the stone and sat on it. 3His face shone like lightning, and his clothing was as white as snow. 4The guards shook with fear when they saw him, and they fell into a dead faint.

5Then the angel spoke to the women. "Don't be afraid!" he said. "I know you are looking for Jesus, who was crucified. 6He isn't here! He has been raised from the dead, just as he said would happen. . . .
MATTHEW 28:1-6

²⁵Jesus told her, "I am the resurrection and the life. Those who believe in me, even though they die like everyone else, will live again. ²⁶They are given eternal life for believing in me and will never perish. . . ."

JOHN 11:25-26

³I passed on to you what was most important and what had also been passed on to me—that Christ died for our sins, just as the Scriptures said. ⁴He was buried, and he was raised from the dead on the third day, as the Scriptures said. ⁵He was seen by Peter and then by the twelve apostles. ⁶After that, he was seen by more than five hundred of his followers at one time. . . . 1 CORINTHIANS 15:3-6

forgiveness Is it ever too late to ask God to forgive me?

Ask God to forgive you *now*, before it's too late. For when Jesus returns (and we don't know when that will be), it *will* be too late to ask him for forgiveness.

²Gather while there is still time, before judgment begins and your opportunity is blown away like chaff. Act now, before the fierce fury of the LORD falls and the terrible day of the LORD's anger begins. ³Beg the LORD to save you—all you who are humble, all you who uphold justice. Walk humbly and do what is right. Perhaps even yet the LORD will protect you from his anger on that day of destruction.

ZEPHANIAH 2:2-3

*¹ Have mercy on me, O God,
        because of your unfailing love.
        blot out the stain of my sins.*

² *Wash me clean from my guilt.*
   Purify me from my sin. PSALM 51:1-2

⁵ *O Lord, you are so good, so ready to forgive,*
   so full of unfailing love for all who ask your
   aid. PSALM 86:5

God Who is God?

God is Spirit. He's the source of all life. That means he isn't a physical being like you or me, limited to one place and time. He's present everywhere, and he sees everything you do. He is everywhere you go, and he hears every word you speak. Not only that, he has shown us what he is like and the way to eternal life.

²⁴*For God is Spirit, so those who worship him must worship in spirit and in truth."* JOHN 4:24

⁴*For the Spirit of God has made me, and the breath of the Almighty gives me life.* JOB 33:4

⁸*"I am the Alpha and the Omega—the beginning and the end," says the Lord God. "I am the one who is, who always was, and who is still to come, the Almighty One."* REVELATION 1:8

Jesus Who is Jesus, anyway?

Jesus is God's Son. God the Father sent him to live thirty-three years on earth, teaching and doing miracles to point people to heaven. Then he allowed Jesus to die on the cross for your sins. However, Jesus didn't stay in the grave—he rose again and now is in heaven with God! Someday he will judge each of us for our actions.

[26]The Father has life in himself, and he has granted his Son to have life in himself. [27]And he has given him authority to judge all mankind because he is the Son of Man. JOHN 5:26-27

[14]. . . the Lord himself will choose the sign. Look! The virgin will conceive a child! She will give birth to a son and will call him Immanuel—"God is with us." ISAIAH 7:14

[6]For a child is born to us, a son is given to us. And the government will rest on his shoulders. These will be his royal titles: Wonderful Counselor, Mighty God, Everlasting Father, Prince of Peace. [7]His ever expanding, peaceful government will never end. He will rule forever with fairness and justice from the throne of his ancestor David. The passionate commitment of the LORD Almighty will guarantee this! ISAIAH 9:6-7

[14]So the Word became human and lived here on earth among us. He was full of unfailing love and faithfulness. And we have seen his glory, the glory of the only Son of the Father. JOHN 1:14

[3]The Son reflects God's own glory, and everything about him represents God exactly. He sustains the universe by the mighty power of his command. After he died to cleanse us from the stain of sin, he sat down in the place of honor at the right hand of the majestic God of heaven. HEBREWS 1:3

prayer Does God really listen when we pray?

Yes, God listens intently to your prayers. He wants you to come to him boldly, so don't be afraid to ask God to meet your needs. But make sure you're thinking about whom you're talking to. Remember, he's the Creator and King of the world! And he promises to give you grace and mercy and to help you when you ask.

16So let us come boldly to the throne of our gracious God. There we will receive his mercy, and we will find grace to help us when we need it. HEBREWS 4:16

7"Keep on asking, and you will be given what you ask for. Keep on looking, and you will find. Keep on knocking, and the door will be opened. 8For everyone who asks, receives. Everyone who seeks, finds. And the door is opened to everyone who knocks."

MATTHEW 7:7-8

11"You fathers—if your children ask for a fish, do you give them a snake instead? 12Or if they ask for an egg, do you give them a scorpion? Of course not! 13If you sinful people know how to give good gifts to your children, how much more will your heavenly Father give the Holy Spirit to those who ask him."

LUKE 11:11-13

14And we can be confident that he will listen to us whenever we ask him for anything in line with his will. 15And if we know he is listening when we make our requests, we can be sure that he will give us what we ask for. 1 JOHN 5:14-15

reverence for God Is it OK to joke about God?

No person on earth can safely defy or make fun of God, the almighty Creator of the universe. He is the one who controls the sun, the galaxies, the mountains, and the length of your life. Why challenge his awesome power? Why risk his judgment? It is much better to give God the reverence and worship he deserves—and experience the blessings of his favor and love!

⁷The LORD is good. When trouble comes, he is a strong refuge. And he knows everyone who trusts in him. ⁸But he sweeps away his enemies in an overwhelming flood. He pursues his foes into the darkness of night. NAHUM 1:7-8

⁵"Do not come any closer," God told him. "Take off your sandals, for you are standing on holy ground." ⁶Then he said, "I am the God of your ancestors—the God of Abraham, the God of Isaac, and the God of Jacob." When Moses heard this, he hid his face in his hands because he was afraid to look at God.

EXODUS 3:5-6

¹⁸Destruction is certain for those who drag their sins behind them, tied with cords of falsehood. ¹⁹They even mock the Holy One of Israel and say, "Hurry up and do something! Quick, show us what you can do. We want to see what you have planned."

ISAIAH 5:18-19

²⁰But the LORD is in his holy Temple. Let all the earth be silent before him." HABAKKUK 2:20

²⁸Since we are receiving a Kingdom that cannot be destroyed, let us be thankful and please God by worshiping him with holy fear and awe. ²⁹For our God is a consuming fire. HEBREWS 12:28-29

salvation Is Christ the only one who can save me?

Jesus didn't say he's *a* way, truth, and life but *the* way, truth, and life. He's your *only* path to God the Father. Think how wonderful it is that God has made it possible for you to be saved! All you have to do is accept it. Then eternal life is yours!

6Jesus told him, "I am the way, the truth, and the life. No one can come to the Father except through me. 7If you had known who I am, then you would have known who my Father is. From now on you know him and have seen him!" JOHN 14:6-7

12But to all who believed him and accepted him, he gave the right to become children of God. 13They are reborn! This is not a physical birth resulting from human passion or plan—this rebirth comes from God. JOHN 1:12-13

16For God so loved the world that he gave his only Son, so that everyone who believes in him will not perish but have eternal life. 17God did not send his Son into the world to condemn it, but to save it.

JOHN 3:16-17

8Salvation that comes from trusting Christ—which is the message we preach—is already within easy reach. In fact, the Scriptures say, "The message is close at hand; it is on your lips and in your heart."

ROMANS 10:8

I'm not perfect. Will God still accept me?

Nobody's perfect—we're all sinners, separated from God. And nobody is good enough to earn his or her way into heaven. But God didn't leave the separation between himself and us. He sent his Son, Jesus, to allow you to be in God's presence if you accept the sacrifice of Christ's death on the cross for your sins.

20God's law was given so that all people could see how sinful they were. But as people sinned more and

more, God's wonderful kindness became more abun-
dant. ROMANS 5:20

*[10]That night Matthew invited Jesus and his disciples
to be his dinner guests, along with his fellow tax
collectors and many other notorious sinners. [11]The
Pharisees were indignant. "Why does your teacher
eat with such scum?" they asked his disciples.*

*[12]When he heard this, Jesus replied, "Healthy peo-
ple don't need a doctor—sick people do." [13]Then he
added, "Now go and learn the meaning of this Scripture: 'I want you to be merciful; I don't want your
sacrifices.' For I have come to call sinners, not those
who think they are already good enough."*

MATTHEW 9:10-13

How can I get to know Jesus?

Becoming a Christian is as close as your own heart
and lips. If you confess that you have sinned (see
"Confession of Sin," page 43), turn away from your
sin, turn to God, and believe in your heart and proclaim with your mouth that Christ is the risen Lord,
then you've become a Christian. Now you can begin
to grow in your relationship with Jesus!

*[9]For if you confess with your mouth that Jesus is
Lord and believe in your heart that God raised him
from the dead, you will be saved. [10]For it is by believing in your heart that you are made right with God,
and it is by confessing with your mouth that you are
saved.* ROMANS 10:9-10

*[38]Peter replied, "Each of you must turn from your
sins and turn to God, and be baptized in the name
of Jesus Christ for the forgiveness of your sins. Then
you will receive the gift of the Holy Spirit. [39]This*

promise is to you and to your children, and even to the Gentiles —all who have been called by the Lord our God." ACTS 2:38-39

¹⁹Now turn from your sins and turn to God, so you can be cleansed of your sins. ²⁰Then wonderful times of refreshment will come from the presence of the Lord, and he will send Jesus your Messiah to you again. ACTS 3:19-20

¹"I am the true vine, and my Father is the gardener. ²He cuts off every branch that doesn't produce fruit, and he prunes the branches that do bear fruit so they will produce even more. ³You have already been pruned for greater fruitfulness by the message I have given you. ⁴Remain in me, and I will remain in you. For a branch cannot produce fruit if it is severed from the vine, and you cannot be fruitful apart from me." JOHN 15:1-4

satan Is Satan real?

Yes, Satan's real—and powerful. He controls those who "refuse to obey God" and do evil. But if you're a Christian, you're no longer a "slave" to Satan. Why? Because God won over Satan when Jesus Christ was raised from the dead. When we obey God and become his children through faith, he gives us the power to win our own battles with Satan and have victory over sin.

²You used to live just like the rest of the world, full of sin, obeying Satan, the mighty prince of the power of the air. He is the spirit at work in the hearts of those who refuse to obey God.

EPHESIANS 2:2

*11Put on all of God's armor so that you will be able
to stand firm against all strategies and tricks of the
Devil. 12For we are not fighting against people made
of flesh and blood, but against the evil rulers and
authorities of the unseen world, against those
mighty powers of darkness who rule this world, and
against wicked spirits in the heavenly realms. . . .
16In every battle you will need faith as your shield to
stop the fiery arrows aimed at you by Satan.*

EPHESIANS 6:11-12, 16

*8Be careful! Watch out for attacks from the Devil,
your great enemy. He prowls around like a roaring
lion, looking for some victim to devour. 9Take a firm
stand against him, and be strong in your faith.
Remember that your Christian brothers and sisters
all over the world are going through the same kind
of suffering you are.* 1 PETER 5:8-9

serving others Should I go out of my way to be kind to others?

Yes! Just hearing about Philemon's opening his heart
and home to Christians made Paul joyful. You can
bring joy and comfort to others, too—the new guy in
your neighborhood, the lonely old lady at church,
the "reject" at school. As you open your home and
heart to others, you show them Christ's love and
"refresh" their hearts.

*6You are generous because of your faith. And I am
praying that you will really put your generosity to
work, for in so doing you will come to an understanding of all the good things we can do for Christ.
7I myself have gained much joy and comfort from*

your love, my brother, because your kindness has so often refreshed the hearts of God's people.

[13]. . . invite the poor, the crippled, the lame, and the blind. [14]Then at the resurrection of the godly, God will reward you for inviting those who could not repay you." LUKE 14:13-14

[16]Don't forget to do good and to share what you have with those in need, for such sacrifices are very pleasing to God. HEBREWS 13:16

taking a stand **I have a hard time taking a stand for Jesus.**

Are you under pressure like Daniel's three friends were? Those guys had guts! They were about to be thrown into a fiery furnace, yet they still stood up to the king and stood strong in their devotion to God. They trusted God to deliver them, but even if he didn't, they wouldn't give up on him. When life gets hot, will *you* be that gutsy?

[16]Shadrach, Meshach, and Abednego replied, "O Nebuchadnezzar, we do not need to defend ourselves before you. [17]If we are thrown into the blazing furnace, the God whom we serve is able to save us. He will rescue us from your power, Your Majesty. [18]But even if he doesn't, Your Majesty can be sure that we will never serve your gods or worship the gold statue you have set up." DANIEL 3:16-18

[28]"Don't be afraid of those who want to kill you. They can only kill your body; they cannot touch your soul. Fear only God, who can destroy both soul and body in hell. [29]Not even a sparrow, worth only half a

penny, can fall to the ground without your Father knowing it. ³⁰And the very hairs on your head are all numbered. ³¹So don't be afraid; you are more valuable to him than a whole flock of sparrows.

MATTHEW 10:28-31

¹⁴*Be happy if you are insulted for being a Christian, for then the glorious Spirit of God will come upon you. ¹⁵If you suffer, however, it must not be for murder, stealing, making trouble, or prying into other people's affairs. ¹⁶But it is no shame to suffer for being a Christian. Praise God for the privilege of being called by his wonderful name!* 1 PETER 4:14-16

witnessing I don't like to talk about my faith.

Once you realize how much God has done for you and you've been filled with the Holy Spirit through faith in Christ, you can't help but want to tell others about Christ and his love. How can you be more bold? Like the disciples (see Acts 4:23-31), you can pray for courage. Then, as the Holy Spirit helps you, look for opportunities to talk about Christ to your friends and neighbors.

¹⁵*I will tell everyone about your righteousness. All day long I will proclaim your saving power. . . .* PSALM 71:15

¹⁸*"If I warn the wicked, saying, 'You are under the penalty of death,' but you fail to deliver the warning, they will die in their sins. And I will hold you responsible, demanding your blood for theirs. ¹⁹If you warn them and they keep on sinning and refuse to repent, they will die in their sins. But you will*

have saved your life because you did what you were told to do." EZEKIEL 3:18-19

[8]So you must never be ashamed to tell others about our Lord. And don't be ashamed of me, either, even though I'm in prison for Christ. With the strength God gives you, be ready to suffer with me for the proclamation of the Good News. 2 TIMOTHY 1:8

[15]. . .if you are asked about your Christian hope, always be ready to explain it. 1 PETER 3:15

[22]Show mercy to those whose faith is wavering. [23]Rescue others by snatching them from the flames of judgment. There are still others to whom you need to show mercy, but be careful that you aren't contaminated by their sins. JUDE 1:22-23

Salvation through  JESUS CHRIST

Here's some great news: God loves you so much that he sent his Son, Jesus Christ, to die in your place and give you life with him forever.

> GOD SO LOVED THE WORLD THAT HE GAVE HIS ONLY SON, SO THAT EVERYONE WHO BELIEVES IN HIM WILL NOT PERISH BUT HAVE ETERNAL LIFE John 3:16

God *longs* for you to accept that sacrifice and become part of his family.

Acknowledge that sin has separated you from God.
The Bible says everyone is sinful: "No one is good—not even one. . . . All have sinned; all fall short of God's glorious standard" (Romans 3:10, 23). You have disobeyed God also, so you will die. God's word says, "The wages of sin is death" (Romans 6:23). Unless something is done, you'll spend eternity in hell, separated from God.

No one deserves eternal life with God in heaven, and no one can do enough good to *earn* God's forgiveness. Instead, God wants you to recognize that you are sinful and to turn to him in trust.

Realize that God has solved the problem of sin.
Jesus died in your place and took the penalty of your
sins, so you don't have to be separated from God in hell
forever. When you put your trust in Jesus Christ to save
you, he gives you eternal life with him. Jesus said, "I am
the resurrection and the life. Those who believe in me,
even though they die like everyone else, will live again"
(John 11:25).

Turn away from your sin, and turn to God.
"If we say we have no sin, we are only fooling ourselves
and refusing to accept the truth. But if we confess our sins
to him, he is faithful and just to forgive us and to cleanse
us from every wrong" (1 John 1:8-9). To receive God's
forgiveness and eternal life, you must confess your sins,
turn away from them, and turn to God.

Here's a short prayer you can pray to help you put your
faith in God:

*Father God, thank you for sending your Son, Jesus Christ,
to die and to rise from the dead to save me. I confess I've
sinned against you. Thank you that Christ paid the penalty
for my sins. I put my trust in you as Savior and Lord. I give
you my life. Thank you for giving me eternal life through
Jesus Christ. Help me to live for you during the rest of my
life on earth. I pray in the name of Jesus, my Savior and
Lord. Amen.*

When you trust Jesus as your Savior, God wipes out all
your sin. You're made perfect in his sight! "He has
brought you back as his friends. He has done this
through his death on the cross in his own human body.
As a result, he has brought you into the very presence of
God, and you are holy and blameless as you stand before
him without a single fault" (Colossians 1:22).

Growing in Faith

"You must continue to believe this truth and stand in it firmly. Don't drift away from the assurance you received when you heard the Good News" (Colossians 1:23).

Read and study your Bible. The Bible is God's own word. The best way to get to know God better and to grow in your faith in him is to read and study the Bible. Spend time every day reading and studying God's book for you!

Pray (talk to God) every day. When you pray, you share your heart and life with God—and God listens! Whatever you are going through, tell God about it. Express your trust with words, and thank him for everything that happens. Tell him about your pains and your struggles. God will walk beside you through everything.

Spend time with other Christians, and worship together. Every Christian is a member of God's family, the "body" of Christ. One of the best ways for you to grow in your faith is to get to know other Christians, to study the Bible with them, and to worship and pray to God with them. This is how God's family grows together as one body.

Share your faith with others. God wants us to tell others about Jesus so that they can have an opportunity to put their trust in him for salvation, too. "Has the Lord redeemed you? Then speak out!" (Psalm 107:2). "Tell everyone about the amazing things he does" (Psalm 96:3). Some will listen, and it's a great joy to see others come to God by faith. "There is joy in the presence of God's angel when even one sinner repents" (Luke 15:10).

In need of prayer?

Call your local church or the National
Counseling Center at 1-800-759-0700.
24 hours A Day, 7 Days A Week.

Visit www.CBNnow.com